FULL METAL PANIC.
05
Original Author SHOUJI GATOU
Art RETSU TATEO
Character Creation SHIKIDOUJI

FULL METAL PANIC!

CONTENTS

MISSION:27 Rescue the two pretty girls!

I've always been required to be perfect…

so I've never done anything stupid…

I know full well the CONSEQUENCES that come with making the wrong decision,

What if something were to happen to me? What about the Danaan and her crew?

but what if I don't do what's expected of me? If I perform my duty less than satisfactorily?

HRMM...

IT LOOKS LIKE THIS ROOM HASN'T BEEN USED IN A LONG TIME.

DARN.

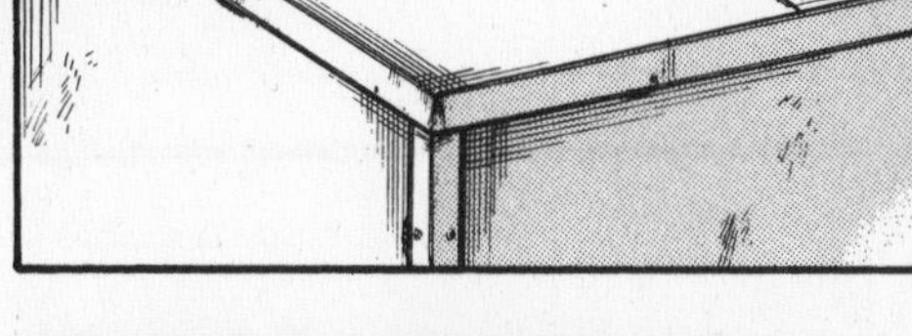

I'm scared…

but things could really go wrong if I stop playing the role of captain…

and go back to being just "Tessa."

EVEN IN EVERYDAY LIFE, THINGS CAN HAPPEN THAT'D MAKE YOU WISH YOU WERE DEAD.
HUH?
BECAUSE OF MY PARENTS' JOBS, I HAD TO LIVE IN AMERICA FOR A WHILE.
WHEN I CAME BACK TO JAPAN, I TRANSFERRED TO A JUNIOR HIGH NEAR BY.
YOU CAN GUESS WHAT HAPPENED NEXT.
I'D GOTTEN INTO THE HABIT OF ALWAYS SAYING WHAT I THOUGHT, AND THE OTHER KIDS DIDN'T LIKE IT AT ALL.
IT WAS HORRIBLE. EVERY DAY WAS HELL.
AND YEAH, I EVEN WANTED TO DIE.
....
IT PROBABLY WOULD'VE BEEN SMARTER FOR ME TO RUN AWAY FROM MY PROBLEMS, BUT I DIDN'T.
AND I THINK I LEARNED A LOT FROM THAT EXPERIENCE.
BESIDES, THINGS ARE COMPLETELY DIFFERENT NOW. I'M HAPPY.
BUT I'D BE EVEN HAPPIER IF THAT **WAR FREAK** WOULD COOL IT.
IS SAGARA **THAT** MUCH OF A NUISANCE?

IT'S LIKE HE'S THROWN COMMON SENSE RIGHT OUT THE WINDOW.
HE DOESN'T MEAN ANY HARM, BUT I DON'T KNOW *WHAT* TO DO WITH HIM.

HE'S PRETTY ROUGH AROUND THE EDGES, BUT HE'S *TRYING.* I CAN'T JUST LEAVE HIM ON HIS OWN.

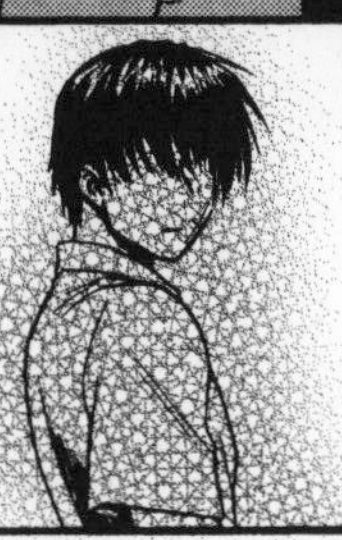
"Rough around the edges…"
Yeah, she may be right.

WHEN I WAS DEPRESSED, AND HE DID HIS BEST TO MAKE ME FEEL BETTER…
I FELT LIKE THAT WAS THE REAL SOSUKE.

I KNOW WHAT YOU MEAN.
I'M *SURE* HE'S ALRIGHT.

YEAH.
YA-CHAK!
ガシャ!
ギ…ギ
CREEAK
OUT.
WE'RE GONNA LET YOU SEE YOUR FRIEND.
TIME FOR A LITTLE MEETING, OLD MAN.
ギイ
CREAK

AUGH!
SHOVE
HUH?
KALININ?
KCHAK
NOW THEN. YOU WOULDN'T WANT...
THIS LITTLE LADY TO GET HURT INSTEAD OF YOU, WOULD YOU?
UNGH

IF NOT, I SUGGEST YOU COOPERATE.
NOW, TELL ME EVERYTHING ABOUT WHO YOU'RE WORKING FOR.
KALININ, DON'T!

FWIP
MAYBE THIS'LL GO QUICKER IF I SHOOT ONE OF HER LEGS, EH?

IT'S CALLED MITHRIL.

OH?
IT'S A MILITARY ORGANIZATION FOUNDED TO COMBAT TERRORISM AND POLITICAL ***DISTURBANCES.***
I'M ASSIGNED TO ITS TACTICAL DIVISION.

YOU KNOW ABOUT THESE GUYS?
I'VE HEARD RUMORS...
HMM.
ALRIGHT, NEXT QUESTION.

HOW MUCH DO YOU KNOW ABOUT THE LAMBDA DRIVER?
TWITCH

I see. She's a tough girl...
YOU BETTER *TALK*...
FINE.
IT...

THE LAMBDA DRIVER...
IS A TECHNOLOGY THAT WE...

WELL. IT LOOKS LIKE YOU'RE IN A LOT OF PAIN. YOUR RIBS MUST BE BROKEN.

...

NOW TALK!
CUZ IF YOU DON'T, THESE GIRLS'LL BE IN A WORLD OF HURT... AND YOU'LL BE DEAD.

IT'S A TECHNOLOGY THAT...
THAT WE...

YO, IT LOOKS LIKE HE'S ABOUT TO DIE.
SHUT YOUR TRAP! WE HAVE TO MAKE HIM TALK BEFORE HE DIES!
THWP
NK
WHA...

BAM!
BAM!
BAM!
BAM!
WHAT THE-?
FWP

BAM!!
I'M GLAD YOU'RE SAFE.
KALININ, YOU'RE HURT!
DON'T WORRY. IT'S NOT ENOUGH TO KILL ME.
THANK GOODNESS. BUT, YOU'RE BLEEDING SO MUCH.
KANAME CHIDORI.
HUH?
Y... YES?

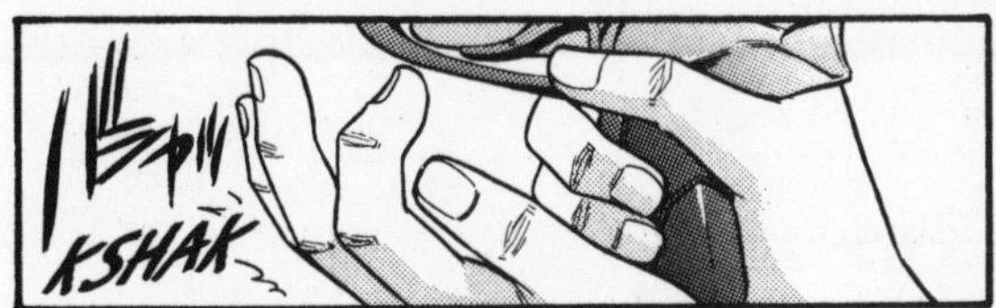

HUH?

C...

CAPTAIN?!

なんですと

WHAT DID HE SAY?

WAIT A MINUTE!
I WANT AN EXPLANATION!
HOW CAN TESSA BE A COMMANDING OFFICER?

I WAS JUST STARTING TO THINK MITHRIL MIGHT NOT BE SO BAD,
BUT NOW I FIND OUT A SIXTEEN YEAR OLD GIRL IS A CAPTAIN?

THIS IS JUST TOO WEIRD!
COMMANDING OFFICERS SHOULD BE TOUGH OLD GUYS LIKE KALININ!

HEY, HOW DID A KLUTZ LIKE HER GET TO BE YOUR SUPERIOR?
I KNOW, BUT...
THAT WAS MEAN...

THERE ARE... CIRCUMSTANCES.

TOK TOK TOK TOK
カン カン カン カン

IT SEEMS THEY'VE NOTICED OUR ESCAPE.
YEAH.

KALININ, I HEARD A NOISE BACK THERE THAT'S GOT ME A LITTLE WORRIED.
WAS IT A GAS TURBINE ENGINE?

YES. IT SOUNDED WAY TOO BIG TO BE AN AS GENERATOR, THOUGH.
IF SOMETHING ON THIS SHIP NEEDS THAT MUCH OUTPUT...
CLUTCH

IT COULD MEAN
THEY HAVE AN INCREDIBLY POWERFUL WEAPON ON BOARD.

WE'LL NEED TO SEARCH THE CARGO HOLD.
BUT CAN WE DO IT?
?
?
?
WE *MUST.*
IF THEY HAVE THAT KIND OF WEAPON, WE HAVE TO DESTROY IT BEFORE THEY CAN ACTIVATE IT.

WRRRRR

WHAT *IS* THAT THING?
IT'S TOO BIG TO BE AN **AS.**

IT'S ENORMOUS!
IF IT GETS MOVING, IT COULD KILL EVERYONE IN ITS PATH!

?!

FLASH

WE CAN'T WASTE ANY TIME!
LOOK FOR THE FUEL TANK AND DESTROY IT!

I KNEW YOU'D SHOW UP HERE.

TAKUMA!
YOU SEEM TO HAVE LOTS OF FRIENDS
WHO'LL COME TO YOUR RESCUE. MUST BE NICE.
...
THIS IS THE BEHEMOTH.
AMAZING, ISN'T IT? AND IT'S NOT *JUST* BIG.
THIS IS NO DIFFERENT THAN NUCLEAR, OR CHEMICAL WEAPONS!
ITS SOLE PURPOSE IS MASS DESTRUCTION!

YES! AND THAT'S ***EXACTLY*** WHAT WE WANT.
THIS IS JUST OUR ***EXPRESSION,*** OUR MEANS TO AN END.
BUT I DON'T UNDERSTAND! WHY WOULD YOU PILOT THAT THING?

WHEN I GET IN THE *BEHEMOTH,* I BECOME INVINCIBLE.
AND IT MAKES MY SISTER HAPPY.

TO TELL YOU THE TRUTH, I KIND OF LIKE YOU.
BUT...

IT'S TIME
TO SAY GOOD-BYE.
BOOM

rrrrumble
AUGH!
WHOA!
OW!
k-chonk
BAM
BAM
BAM
BAM
BAM
BAM
AAUGH!
WHAT ... WHAT'S GOING ON?
HUFF
RRRRR
WHERE'S KALININ?
DID HE GO THE OTHER WAY?
BA-BANG BAM BAM

ゴゴゴ
RRRUMBLE
YEAH, BUT HOW CAN I GET OUT OF HERE BY MYSELF?
HUFF
HUFF
GASP
はっ
An enemy?
He's coming this way!
WHY ...
DOES THIS ALWAYS HAPPEN TO ME?
LUNGE
FWSH
BWAP

SLIP
OH!
HUH?
YOU'RE MORE CAPABLE THAN I THOUGHT.
SOSUKE!

MISSION:28 [A place for Takuma]

He's alive!

CHIDORI.

ARE YOU HURT?

Sosuke's alive!

He keeps me waiting for so long…
And then he just shows up out of the blue!
He has no idea how that makes me feel!

Thank God he's safe…
MISSION:28 A Place for Takuma

I WAS SO WORRIED ABOUT YOU!
I WAS SO SCARED!
I'M SORRY.
IT TOOK A WHILE TO GET THE BOMB IN PLACE.

WHA..?
BAM
HA HA.
I GUESS THIS ISN'T THE TIME TO CELEBRATE.
UUUGH..
SAGARA!

THIS WAY!
HURRY!
BAM
BAM
CAPTAIN!
I'M SORRY FOR TAKING SO LONG.
NO,
I'M THE ONE WHO SHOULD APOLOGIZE.

I THOUGHT YOU WERE...
GASP

I'M GLAD THAT YOU'RE SAFE.
SMILE

rub rub

LIEU-TENANT COM-MANDER.
I'LL EXPLAIN LATER.
YOU HAVE TO GET THESE TWO OUT OF HERE FIRST.

AM GOING TO KEEP THEM FROM ACTIVATING THIS MACHINE.

That's right…

There are people who accept me, and trust me as their commanding officer.

I have to…

AUGH!

TAKUMA!

DON'T JUST SIT THERE! GET IN THE *BEHEMOTH!*

GRAB

I WILL, BUT...

I'M BLEEDING. I NEED TO HAVE THIS LOOKED AT.

YOU'RE NOT HURT SO BAD THAT YOU CAN'T ***PILOT!*** NOW GET UP!

IF YOU DON'T GET THE *BEHEMOTH* MOVING, YOU'LL RUIN ***EVERYTHING*** WE'VE BEEN WORKING FOR!

I ***KNOW*** HOW IMPORTANT THIS IS TO YOU, SIS...

BUT I'M ***HURT!*** IF I PILOT IT LIKE THIS...

SHOVE

AUGH!

STOP BEING SUCH A BABY!

IF YOU'RE NOT GOING TO PILOT THE *BEHEMOTH*, THEN YOU'RE ***USELESS!***

WE DON'T NEED YOU ANYMORE!

All she ever cared about was the *Behemoth*. That ***MONSTER.***

...PRICK
......
I'M GETTING IN, SIS.
KSHANG

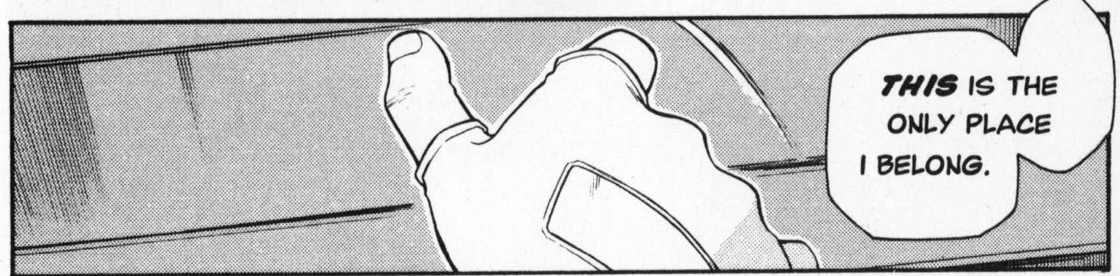
THIS IS THE ONLY PLACE I BELONG.

HOLD IT RIGHT THERE.

NOW WALK TOWARDS ME, **SLOWLY**.
HMM, WHAT SHOULD I DO?
THERE'S NOWHERE ELSE TO GO.
I'LL SHOOT, EVEN IF YOU **ARE** A KID.
SQUEEZE
BA-
SKREE
PUT THE GUN DOWN.
EVEN IF YOU DO PILOT THAT THING...
IT STILL WON'T CHANGE ANYTHING.

I KNOW.
BAM
......!

SGGH
HRNG...
STAGGER
RRRUMBLE
DAMN!
TAKUMA!
RRRUMBLE
!!
GET IN THE BEHEMOTH!
YOU...

ARE A PART OF THE BEHEMOTH!
SNAP
CRACK
ROAR
SNAP
KER-KRUNCH!

RRRUMBLE
YAUGH!
CAPTAIN, ARE YOU ALRIGHT?
Y... YEAH.
So Sosuke had been calling her "Miss Tessa" to hide her identity…
She really **IS** his commanding officer.
But…
why doesn't that make me feel any better?
Even if they **ARE** commander and subordinate…
they **STILL** might possibly be…
SHAKE SHAKE
Urgh! Stop it! Stop it!

This is **NOT** the time to be thinking about that kind of thing.
RRRUMBLE
はっ
HUH?
BLUSH

YO!
POINK!
ひょいっ
SHWIP

DON'T SNEAK UP ON ME LIKE THAT!
I WAS ABOUT TO *SHOOT* YOU!
ALRIGHT, ALRIGHT.
HUP!
WEBER!
KURZ?
IN THE FLESH!
HOW ARE YOU CUTE LITTLE LADIES DOING?

WHOOPS.
THIS PART'S SINKING TOO, HUH?
IT'S GOING DOWN FASTER THAN WE THOUGHT...
WAUGH
SORRY, MAN. BOMBS AREN'T EXACTLY MY SPECIALTY.
OH, WAS *THAT* IT?
YEAH!
I'M A *SNIPER*, BORN AND BRED!
WHAT A WEIRD CONVERSATION...
ALRIGHT! IT'S THE DECK!
SPLISSH
SPLOOOSH

EEEEEK!
RRRUMBLE
HUP!
TOK!
TWUMP
ALRIGHT!
YOU'RE NEXT, CAPTAIN!
OKAY ...
ba-dump
ba-dump
TWUMP

WHOA!
GOTCHA.

TWUMP!
NEXT!

......
SPIN
くるっ
THANKS, KURZ!

DAMN.
WHAT'S WRONG?

ALRIGHT!
MISSION COMPLETE! AND THAT'S THAT FOR THE EVIL FORTRESS!
HA!
RRRUMBLE
I'M WORRIED.
KALININ MIGHT STILL BE IN THERE...

WHA?!

THE OLD DUDE'S STILL ALIVE?

OF COURSE! DON'T COUNT HIM FOR DEAD *YET!*

URZU 7 TO URZU 2.

beep

URZU 2 HERE.

WHY DIDN'T YOU ASK ME THAT *SOONER?*

IS THE LIEUTENANT COMMANDER STILL INSIDE THE SHIP? PLEASE CONFIRM.

WHAT?!

KONG
K-CHONG
!!?
SKRASH!

WHAAM!

WHA-

AA...
AUGH...
OH MY GOD!

MISSION:29 [Last Wish]
WHA...
WHAT THE HELL IS THAT?

MISSION:29 Last Wish

URZU 2! BUY US SOME TIME TO GET OUT OF HERE.

IT'S TOO BIG... I CAN'T TELL WHAT IT IS.

THE ***SIZE*** OF THAT THING...

MY **AI** CAN'T EVEN CALCULATE

ROGER!

HOW AM I GOING TO TAKE IT ON?

HMPF.

BWOOSH

FWAM
WHA?!
WHAT IS THIS THING, FRIDAY?
ERROR IN LOWER DRIVE TRAIN.
CRACK!!

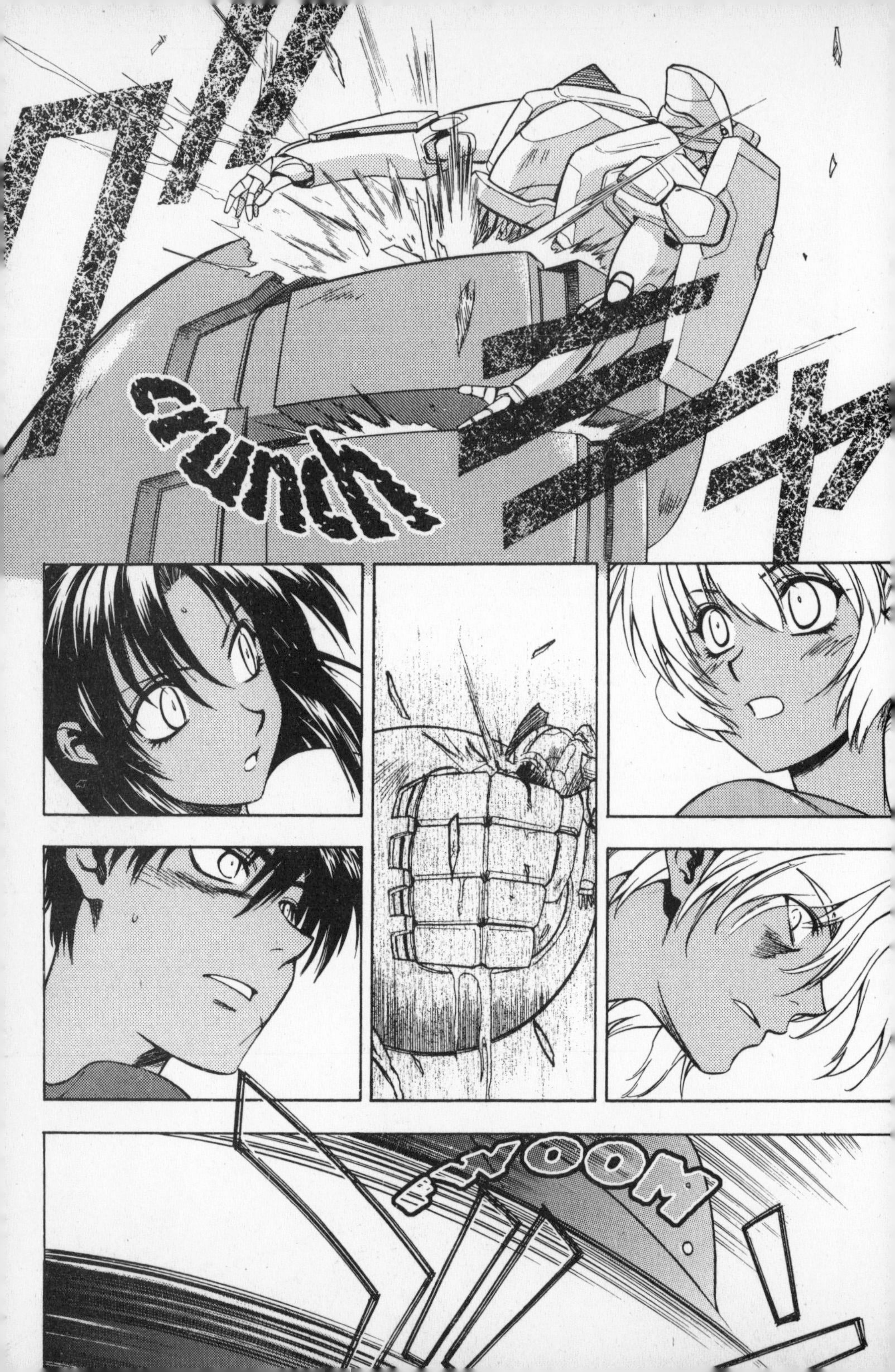
Punch
FWOOM

SPLOOSH
ME...
MELISSA!
MAO!
COME ON!
WE HAVE TO GET THESE TWO OUT OF HERE FIRST.
...
I KNOW HOW YOU FEEL, BUT WE HAVE TO LEAVE OR WE'LL **ALL** BE KILLED.
AND BESIDES...

IT'S NOT LIKE WE AIN'T ***USED*** TO THIS KINDA WORK!
3
GLUBB
2

1

SPLOOOSH!

SPLISSH

SAGARA, GIVE ME A COMMUNICATOR!

MA'AM.

SLAM!
HUP
UM, *THIS* IS OUR GETAWAY CAR?
THIS IS AN EMERGENCY.
CAPTAIN, WHAT ARE YOUR ORDERS?
RIGHT NOW, JUST GET US AWAY FROM THE PIER.
WE'LL COME UP WITH A PLAN *AFTER* WE'VE CONTACTED THE *DANAAN.*
ROGER.
THIS IS TESTAROSSA. PATCH ME THROUGH TO COMMANDER MARDUKAS! THIS IS TOP PRIORITY!
beep
ROGER.
FIVE SECONDS, PLEASE.
SCREE
VROOOOM
If Takuma had been killed instead of Kalinin, the *Behemoth* wouldn't have been activated.
And we wouldn't have lost Melissa like that.

I'm not perfect.

But that doesn't mean I can just give up.

CAPTAIN! YOU'RE SAFE!

MARDUKAS!

WHERE IS THE SHIP NOW?

120 KM OFF THE KII PENINSULA.

No good!

That's too far away!

It would take about two hours for reinforcements to get here. And they're out of range to use boosters.

We could launch the same kind of missile we used in Sunan in about an hour, but we can't wait that long.

Isn't there...

anything else we can do?

CAPTAIN.

DO YOU NEED AN ARBALEST IMMEDIATELY?

That's right.
I'm not going to give up.

KANAME!
ARE THERE ANY BIG BUILDINGS AROUND HERE, LIKE AN EXHIBITION HALL OR SOMETHING?
HUH?
SURE. OVER THERE ON YOUR RIGHT.
IT'S CALLED "TOKYO BIG SIGHT."
PERFECT!

DAMN ...
DAMN IT!
WHEN I...
SPLOOSH
KA-THUD
AM IN THE BEHEMOTH,
I AM INVINCIBLE!
CHING

BOOM
BOOM
BOOM
BOOM
BOOM
BOOM
BOOM
BOOM
BOOM
!!
WHAT WAS THAT?
OH NO. THAT THING IS WALKING!
SCRUNCH
UH, IS IT JUST ME...

OR DOES IT LOOK LIKE HE'S SPOTTED US?
THWOOM
BOOM
BAM
BAM
BAM
AAAAUGH!
SCREEEEEE
TH... TH...THE ASPHALT!
HANG ON TO SOMETHING! I'M GOING TO SPEED UP!
SOSUKE!

I'M GONNA BUY US SOME TIME, BUT YOU HAVE TO DRIVE ABSOLUTELY STRAIGHT!
AND DON'T CHANGE YOUR SPEED, EITHER!
GOT IT.

H...HEY, WHAT'RE YOU GOING TO DO?
DON'T WORRY.

HE WON'T LET US DOWN.

ALRIGHT.
YOUR TURN, BABY.

COME AND GET ME, BUCKET-HEAD.
BANG

CHING
BOOM
ALRIGHT! BULLSEYE!
WHOA! HOW DID YOU DO THAT, KURZ?
AAH, IT WAS NO BIG DEAL.
WA HA HA HA HA!
I JUST PUT SOME "GARBAGE" IN ITS MUZZLE BEFORE IT FIRED.
NOW'S OUR CHANCE TO GET AS FAR AWAY FROM IT AS WE CAN!
RIGHT!

......?

WAS IT YOU?
YEAH.
KINDA STUPID OF ME, HUH?

HOW DID I GET TO SHORE?

BEHEMOTH IS ON THE MOVE.
YOU'VE WON.
....

IT HAS ENOUGH FUEL TO RUN FOR FORTY HOURS.
UNTIL THAT RUNS OUT, ***NOTHING*** CAN STOP IT.
NONE OF THIS MATTERS ANYMORE, SO I MIGHT AS WELL TELL YOU...

THE *BEHEMOTH* WAS CREATED TO HUNT DOWN REGULAR **AS** UNITS.
THAT'S WHY WE NEEDED THE LAMBDA DRIVER,
AND TAKUMA TO CONTROL IT.

YOU KNOW, I'M NOT EVEN HIS SISTER.
HE JUST STARTED BELIEVING I WAS AFTER HE ***KILLED*** HIS REAL SISTER.
I USED THAT TO MY OWN ADVANTAGE.
HEH. I LOST ***MY*** FAMILY A LONG TIME AGO.
AND I'VE BEEN LIVING ON MY OWN EVER SINCE.

BWOOOM!

DO YOU KNOW WHY I SAVED YOU?
I THINK I HAVE AN IDEA.
HA!

HEY, FATHER.
COULD YOU AT LEAST TELL ME YOUR NAME?

WHEN YOU TALK LIKE THAT, YOU SOUND WISE AND ALL-KNOWING.
LIKE A PRIEST OR SOMETHING.

ANDREI SERGEIVICH KALININ.
HEH.
THAT'S A...
STRANGE NAME...

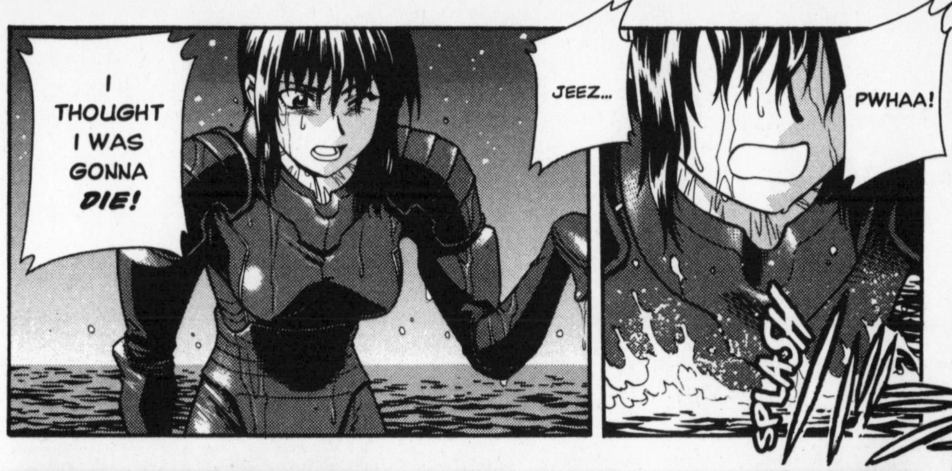
PWHAA!
SPLASH
JEEZ...
I THOUGHT I WAS GONNA *DIE!*

HUH?

LIEU-TENANT COM-MANDER.
DO YOU KNOW HER?

YES.

BOOM

STOMP

BAM
BAM
BAM
BAM
BAM
BAM
BAM

UGH. ALL THIS *EXCITEMENT* IS MAKING ME SICK TO MY STOMACH.
!!

WOOOOOOO
I SEE IT!
OUR REINFORCEMENTS?
CHING
BAM
BOOM
BOOM
BOOM
!!

AAAAUGH!
DON'T WORRY. IT WON'T GET DESTROYED THAT EASILY.
SAGARA!
WE'LL USE THE TRUCK AS A DECOY WHILE YOU GET INTO THE ARBALEST.
BUT
MA'AM ...
TAKE THE WHEEL, CHIDORI.
WHA...
WHAAT?
DON'T WORRY ABOUT ME!
IT'S YOU THAT WE'RE ALL COUNTING ON!
YOU'VE GOTTA BE KIDDING! I DON'T EVEN HAVE A LICENSE!
WOULDN'T IT BE BETTER IF KURZ...
THANKS.
SOSUKE!
SHWASH!!

FINE!
BUT IF SOMETHING HAPPENS, DON'T BLAME ME!
THMP
I'M JUST A HIGH SCHOOL KID! I SHOULDN'T BE DRIVING!
SKSH
SKSH
SKSH

MISSION:30 At the end of the battle

SCREEEEEEEE

UGH!

WHA?
FROM THE SIDE!
BAM BAM BAM BAM
SKRASH!

LOOM
WAAAAAUGH!
BWOOOM!
KANAME! IF WE STAY OUT IN THE OPEN, WE'RE GONNA GET **SHOT!**
BUST THROUGH THAT SHUTTER OVER THERE!
WHAT?!
HYAAA!
BA-BOOM!
HERE GOES!
VWOOOM

CRASH!
Scree
Screeee
MY...
MY HEAD.
Screeee
Scree

VRRRRRR
UNHH...
TOK
タン..
TESSA!
HEY, ARE YOU ALRIGHT?
HURRY...
HAVE TO GET AWAY...
TREMBLE
CRUNCH
ギ

SKRKKKKKK

Looks like it's MY turn again.

HMPH.
THEN I'LL JUST KILL YOU ALL FIRST!
BA-BOOM!
ROOOOAR
WHA ...
?!

オォ
オォ
オ
オォ
FWOOOOO...
YOU CALLED?

THERE YOU ARE...

SOSUKE SAGARA!

FWEEN
BOOM BOOM BOOM
!!
THAT'S...
BOOM BOOM BOOM BOOM
TOO BAD, YOU CAN'T TOUCH ME!
AHAHA!
SHKRANK
BOOM BOOM

WOOOOOOO
A LAMBDA DRIVER!
JUST LIKE THAT TIME IN SUNAN!

Impossible. He doesn't know a THING.

MURMUR
MURMUR
MURMUR
Hey, look.
This time...
SHWP
SHWP
SHWP
you should give your body to ME.
Ahahahaha! If you do, no one will die.
That is,
AAAAUGH!
so long as YOU'RE the one who disappears.

STOP THIS, NOW!
ZWOOSH
I will NOT allow you to just do whatever you want! Now go away!
HUH?
WHO... WHO ARE YOU?
That's not important right now. There's something you need to tell Sosuke, and quickly!
He has to destroy the Lambda Driver's coolant system.
HUH?
SHWP
Hurry!
The only one who can save him is YOU.

KANAME! GOOD, YOU'RE AWAKE!

YOU WERE HAVING SOME SORT OF ***NIGHTMARE.***

KURZ! GIVE ME YOUR COMMUNICATOR!

AND TELL ME WHERE THE COOLANT SYSTEM IS!

FWIP

THE COOLANT SYSTEM?
WHA?
...?
WHA-
BOOM
Concen-
trate…
Picture
my
shots
piercing
his
armor,
SKRSSH
then
focus
that
image…
CHAK
into
the
bullets!
BAM
BAM

SH-POW!
BOOM
GOT HIM!
BA-BOOM
TOTTER
あ
Shit!
It still didn't do enough damage.

BA-BOOM
HUFF
HUFF
THERE!
THAT ROUND PART, AND THE BIG THING ON ITS BACK!
SOSUKE, CAN YOU HEAR ME?
CHI-DORI?
WHAT IS IT?
GOT IT!
THANKS, KURZ!
beep

THAT THING'S WEAK POINT IS THE COOLANT SYSTEM FOR THE LAMBDA DRIVER!
USE ***YOUR*** LAMBDA DRIVER AND AIM FOR THAT SPOT!
WHAT?!
AIM WHERE? THERE'S MORE THAN ONE COOLANT SYSTEM!

OOMPH!
FWOMP
SKIDDD

It's alright.
You can do it.
IT'S THE BIG SLIT ON ITS BACK!
ONE SHOT SHOULD BE ENOUGH!
GOT IT!
WHOOSH
BA-KOOM
Concentrate ...
SPIN

SLIIIIIIDE

CRAP.

Picture my shots piercing his armor…

GO TO HELL!
BA-CHING
SHPOW!

ガ
rumble
rumble
ガ
ガガ
rumble
rumble
ガ
ガ
K-RACK
ズ
skrsssh
ド
ザ
ガ
ガ
ガ
rumble
ガ
ガ
ガガ
ガ
ビキ
TER-SKRACK!
ビキ
ガ
SKRACK

SNAP
KRA-SNAP
SKRUNCH
TOTTER
CRKKCRKK
SNAP

ZKRSHH

...
OH!
TESSA,
ARE YOU AL-RIGHT?

S...
SIS.
I HAVE...
NO-THING LEFT.
OH.
すっ SHP
NO-THING.
姉さん……！
SIS!

WELL THEN,
GOOD WORK, EVERYONE!
THAT WAS AN EXCEL-LENT SHOT, WEBER!
YEAH, I GUESS.

SAGARA.
THE ARBALEST IS YOURS NOW.
M...
MA'AM?
PLEASE TAKE CARE OF IT.

AND KANAME.
HM?

I HAVE TO THANK YOU, TOO.
AND I'M SORRY ABOUT EVERYTHING YOU'VE BEEN PUT THROUGH.
YOU SHOULD BE! ANY OTHER GIRL PROBABLY WOULD'VE **DIED!**

BUT TESSA, FOR SOMEONE WHO SAYS THEY'RE CLUMSY, YOU SURE TRIED HARD, TOO!
OF COURSE, YOU KINDA RAN OUT OF STEAM IN THE END...
AHAH.
IS THAT RIGHT?

IN PART-ICULAR,

SPIN

WHEN YOU TOLD ME **THOSE THINGS** BACK THEN, YOU MADE ME SO HAPPY.

I'M GOING TO COME SEE YOU AGAIN!

WHAT DO YOU MEAN, "BACK THEN"?

AND WHAT **THINGS** ARE YOU TALKING ABOUT?

WELL THEN, I SUPPOSE WE SHOULD MOVE OUT...

C'MON, TELL ME!

MISSION:31 [Sweet Memories]

By the age of six,
I had solved Einstein's Field Equations.

In my early teens,
I designed the assault submarine
the *Tuatha de Danaan.*

And then,
I was placed in command of the *Danaan*
and her crew of 250 people.

IT'S HOT.
But right now, I have no idea where I am or what I should do.

MISSION:31 Sweet Memories

Sorry Yang, but I'll be taking this opportunity to do something for **MYSELF**.

Besides, I've always wanted to take a train trip on my own.

Please be careful.

Yes, ma'am.

CLACK CLACK CLACK CLACK CLACK CLACK

SIGH.

I'M TIRED.

I COULDN'T REALLY GET MUCH SLEEP, WHAT WITH TODAY'S MEETING AND ALL.
DROOP
I GUESS I SHOULD REST NOW WHILE I CAN...
CLACK CLACK
ゴトン
ゴトン
CLACK CLACK

EXCUSE ME, MISS.
LAST STOP.
GASP
はっ
HOW LONG HAVE I BEEN ASLEEP?
OH NO!

EX-CUSE ME!

YES?
WHEN IS THE NEXT TRAIN?

......
NO MORE OUTBOUND TRAINS TODAY.
WHA ?!

I HATE TO ADMIT IT, BUT I GUESS I SHOULD CALL FOR HELP.

BEEP

HISSSSSSSS
TWICTH

OUT OF SATELLITE RANGE?!
AAAUGH!

I CAN'T BELIEVE I JUST FELL ASLEEP LIKE THAT.
AND I SHOULD'VE CHECKED WHETHER THE COMMUNICATOR WOULD WORK BEFORE I LEFT.
MISS?
AAAUGH

IS SOMETHING WRONG?

WELL,
UM,
I SORT OF MISSED MY STOP...
AND THE STATION ATTENDANT SAID THERE WON'T BE ANY MORE TRAINS TODAY.

IS THERE A PLACE AROUND HERE I CAN SPEND THE NIGHT?
NOPE.

HOP IN.

HELLO THERE, DEAR!

MY HUSBAND TOLD ME WHAT HAPPENED. HOW HORRIBLE!

WE DON'T HAVE MUCH, BUT YOU'RE WELCOME TO STAY!

HAHAHAHAHAHA!

AHAHAHAHA!

I'M SORRY FOR IMPOSING.

SIGH

MY NAME IS

TELETHA TESTAROSSA.

THAT'S QUITE A NAME.

TESA... TERROTH?

BOW

MAYBE I'LL JUST CALL YOU "TESSY."

WOULD YOU MIND THAT?

NO, NOT AT ALL.

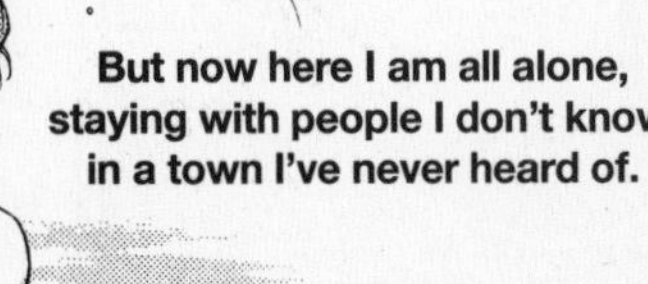

HEH.

IT'S ALMOST LIKE I'M **DREAMING.**

THERE YOU GO!
PAT
ぽん
MY, IT LOOKS PER-FECT!
LIKE IT WAS MADE JUST FOR YOU!
TAKE A LOOK, DEAR!
DOESN'T MASAKO'S OLD YUKATA LOOK GREAT ON HER?
YEAH.
WHAT ARE YOU, SHY?
BWSH
ばし
ばし
ばし
BWSH
BWSH
WHY DON'T YOU SAY SOMETHIN' NICE?
あはははは
AHAHAHAHA
These two...
are a little like Sagara and Kaname

THE STARS LOOK SO BEAUTI- FUL...
MM- HMM.

THAT'S CUZ THE AIR'S NICE AND CLEAN HERE.

'COURSE... THAT'S ABOUT ALL WE GOT HERE.
Why does this all...
AHAHAHA
あははははは

feel so familiar?
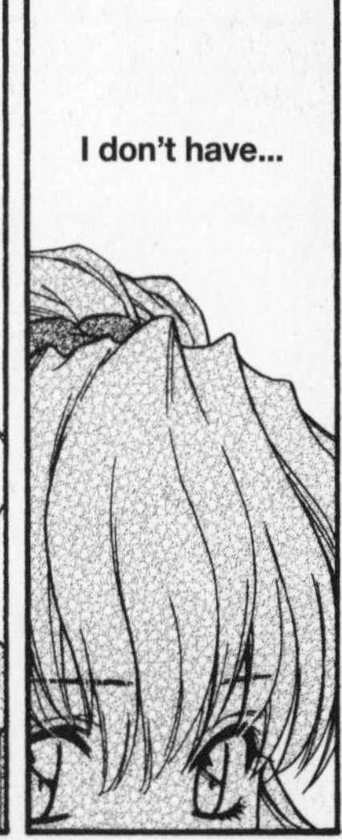
I don't have...

ANY memories like this, and yet...

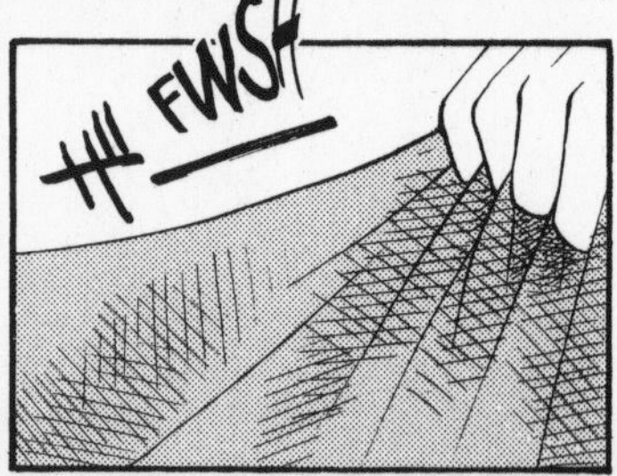

MOSQUITO NET 蚊帳。

READY, TESSY?
LET'S GO.

WOW!

LOOK AT ALL THE SUN-FLOWERS!
AREN'T THEY PRET-TY?
THEY JUST ALL OF A SUDDEN OPENED UP.

ANYHOW, FIRST WE HAVE TO WEED THE FIELDS.
JUST WALK AROUND AND PULL WHATEVER YOU CAN.

SEEIN' THESE FLOWERS BLOOM LIKE THIS...
KINDA CHEERS ME UP, YOU KNOW?
YEAH.

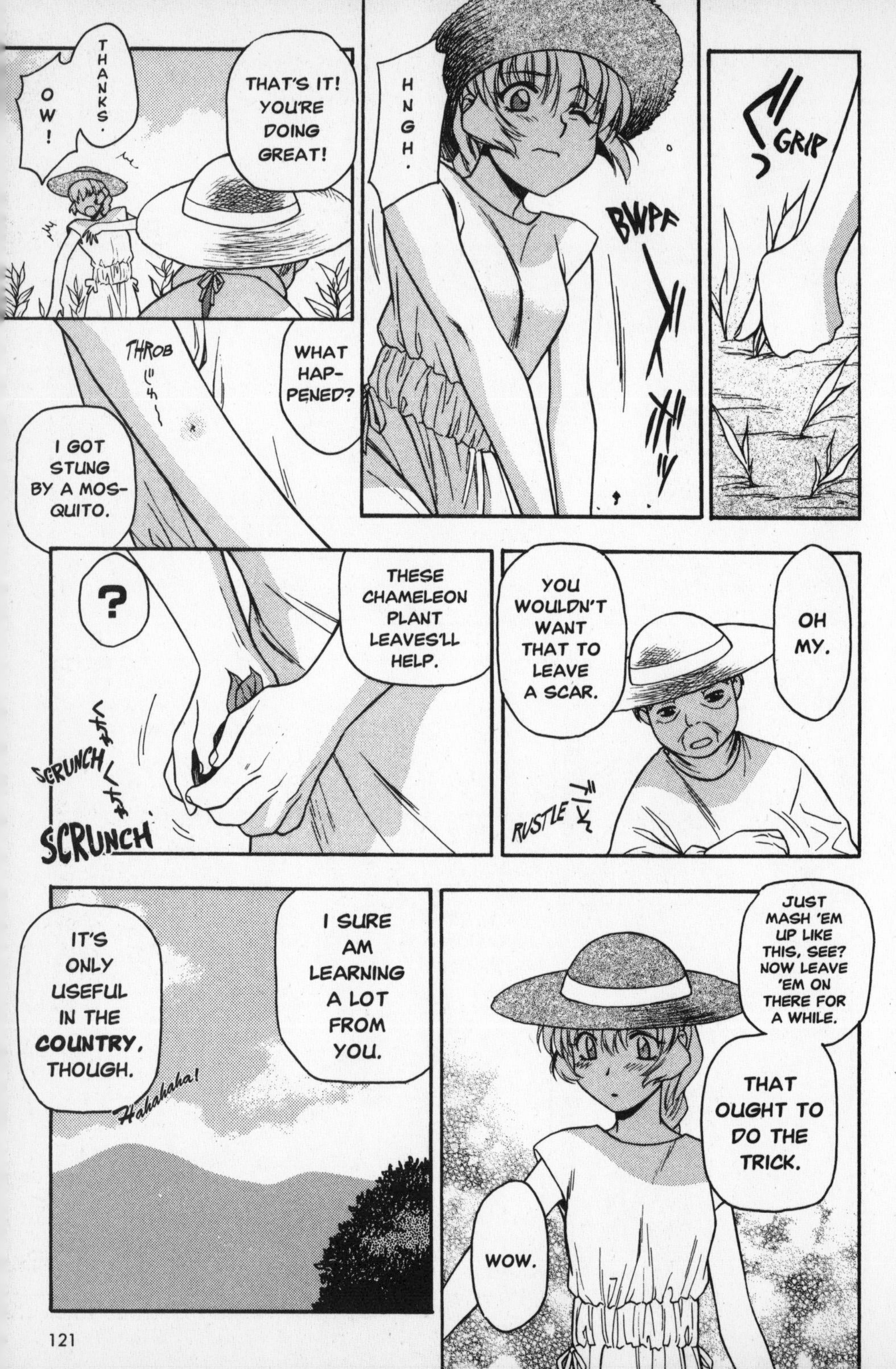
GRIP
BWPF
HNGH.
THAT'S IT! YOU'RE DOING GREAT!
THANKS. OW!
WHAT HAP-PENED?
THROB
I GOT STUNG BY A MOS-QUITO.
OH MY.
YOU WOULDN'T WANT THAT TO LEAVE A SCAR.
RUSTLE
THESE CHAMELEON PLANT LEAVES'LL HELP.
?
SCRUNCH
SCRUNCH
JUST MASH 'EM UP LIKE THIS, SEE? NOW LEAVE 'EM ON THERE FOR A WHILE.
THAT OUGHT TO DO THE TRICK.
WOW.
I SURE AM LEARNING A LOT FROM YOU.
IT'S ONLY USEFUL IN THE COUNTRY, THOUGH.
Hahahaha!

AAHH.
I GIVE UP.
OH.
WHY DON'T YOU LET ME TAKE A LOOK AT IT?

GOOD NEWS!
TOK

TESSY!

I WONDER WHERE SHE WENT OFF TO.
AND I JUST CUT SOME WATER-MELON, TOO.
......

I FIXED YOUR TRUCK!
THERE WAS JUST A CLOG IN THE OIL LINE.

SMILE

HERE.

GO ON AND GET WASHED.
WE CAN'T HAVE A PRETTY GIRL LIKE YOU ALL MUSSED UP...

THANK YOU.

REEREE
REEREE
IT SHOULD BE DRY BY THE TIME YOU LEAVE.
THANK YOU. IT MUST'VE BEEN HARD GETTING ALL THAT OIL OFF.
IT WAS THE LEAST I COULD DO!

REEREE
REEREE
YOU KNOW,
WHEN I LEAVE TOMOR-ROW...

I'll be going back to my job, and all the **responsibilities** that come with it.

The lives of many people will be in my hands.

It's what I wanted to do, though, so I don't have any regrets. Still...

Surrounded by plants and wildlife...

YOU JUST STAY THE WAY YOU ARE...

AND NO MATTER WHAT HAPPENS, YOU'LL DO FINE.

living close to the land...

If I hadn't been born a Whispered...

I think **THIS** is the kind of life I would've had.

I REALLY ENJOYED IT.
THANK YOU BOTH SO VERY MUCH!
OUR PLEASURE. IT'S BEEN A WHILE SINCE WE'VE HAD A **VISITOR.**
KER-CLANK
BE CARE-FUL!
TESSY!
I'M SURE YOU'LL FIND A PLACE CLOSE TO YOUR HEART, JUST LIKE THIS ONE!
YOU'LL BE FINE!
Oh, sir...

THANK YOU!

I WON'T FORGET YOU!

Oh no.

I'm falling asleep again.

IT ISN'T EVEN ON THE MAP ANY MORE.

IT WAS **FLOODED** FIVE YEARS AGO, DURING CONSTRUCTION OF A LOCAL DAM.

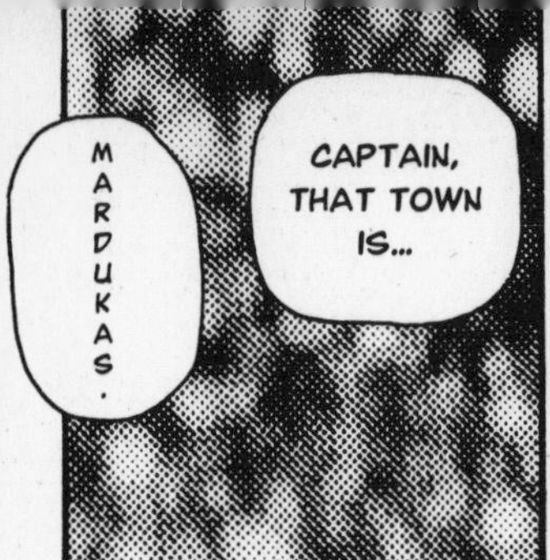

It felt so familiar, so comfortable.

I've never been anywhere like that before, so I **SHOULDN'T** have those kinds of feelings inside of me...

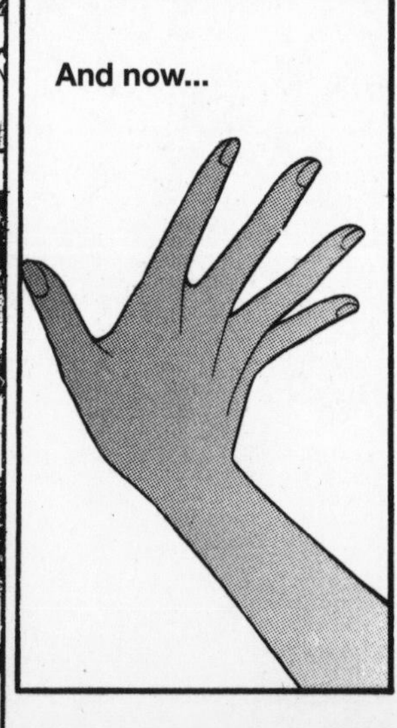

I feel I can move forward again. Not as a sixteen year old girl, but as the CAPTAIN of the *Danaan*.

And...

VERY WELL. LET ME HAVE YOUR REPORT.
MA'AM!
CHK

MISSION:32 The Long road to the vacation house

IT'S SUMMER...
ZWEE
ZWEEE
ZWEE

ZWEE
ZWEE
ZWEE
AND THE GANG'S ALL HERE!

HWEE
HWEE
IT'S SUMMER, BUT I CAN HEAR NIGHTINGALES.
WELL, WE **ARE** OUT IN THE WILDERNESS...
セミと一緒に…
ALONG WITH THE CICADAS
LAST SUMMER, OUR TRIP TO THE BEACH ENDED IN DISASTER.
BUT THIS YEAR WE'RE GOING TO A FRIEND'S VACATION HOUSE, AND IT'S GONNA BE **GREAT**!
SAGARA! HEY, SAGARA!

ALTHOUGH I'M A LITTLE WORRIED SINCE **HE'S** WITH US.
ISN'T YOUR BAG HEAVY?
STUFFED
NOT A PROBLEM. IT'S ONLY AROUND TWENTY POUNDS.
WHAT?
TWENTY POUNDS?
BUT ISN'T THAT **HEAVY?**
BESIDES, THIS AREA HAS A FAVORABLE CLIMATE,
SO THERE'S NO NEED TO WORRY ABOUT GETTING WASHED OUT BY HUMIDITY OR RAIN.
NOT LISTENING
IN MYANMAR, WE-
SPIN
くるくるくる
SPIN
SPIN
SPIN
BWACK!
I **TOLD** YOU TO KEEP THOSE KINDS OF STORIES TO YOURSELF, DIDN'T I?
LIKE, SEVERAL CHAPTERS AGO.
OH
OH
OH

LOOK, WE'RE NOT IN SOME MERCENARY CAMP, ALRIGHT? AAH, WHATEVER.
JUST MAKE SURE YOU DON'T **BOTHER** ANYONE. ♡
EEEK!
WHAT **IS** THAT?!
SHIORI?
SOME-THING'S ON MY BACK!
I'M SCARED!
SHWP

IT'S JUST A BEETLE.
NO PROB-LEM.
YOU'RE THE PROBLEM, YOU DOLT!
SLAM!
IT'S ALRIGHT, SHIORI. HE DIDN'T MEAN ANYTHING BY IT!
うわあああああん
Crying like a baby
JUST FORGET IT EVER HAPPENED, ALRIGHT?!
HYAA!
DAMMIT, SAGARA!
DO YOU THINK YOU CAN JUST DO WHATEVER YOU WANT?
I SAW SHIORI'S BRA...
WAAAUCH!
IF WE WERE IN THE MATRIX,
I'D INSTALL SOME COMMON SENSE INTO THAT THICK SKULL OF YOURS!
TWITCH
TWITCH
TWITCH
AS PUNISHMENT, GO FIND A PLACE WHERE WE CAN STOP AND EAT SOME SNACKS!
AND IT BETTER NOT BE SOME RANDOM TUFT OF GRASS!
YEAH! YEAH!
オーオー
Serves him right!
UNDER-STOOD.

I CAN'T BELIEVE THAT **SAGARA** FOUND A NICE SPOT BY A LAKE.

MAYBE THE TOUGH GUY'S A **ROMANTIC** AT HEART.

STOP! YOU'RE MAKING ME BLUSH!

SPEAKING OF WHICH, I WONDER WHERE OUR "ROMANTICIST" WENT OFF TO?

He said he was getting something ready...

何か準備するって言って……

UH...

I DON'T REMEMBER.

エヘッ EH HEH

YOU DON'T REMEMBER?!

なッ WHA?

HEY, HOW MUCH FURTHER 'TIL WE GET TO THE HOUSE?

I HAVEN'T BEEN THERE SINCE I WAS A KID.

MY DAD DREW ME A MAP, THOUGH.

RUSTLE ガサ

Here. *CALL ME if you get lost!

ここ ※迷ったら電話しろ!! Tel:

湖 Lake

Station 駅

Something a kid would draw

小学生並み。

YOU DON'T, DO YOU?
DO YOU?
WE'RE IN THE MOUNTAINS! DO YOU SEE ANY ANTENNAS OUT HERE?!
RATTLE RATTLE
HEY, IT'S ALRIGHT! IF WE GET LOST, WE CAN JUST CALL!
YOU GOTTA BE KIDDIN'.
YEAH...
KANA, I DON'T THINK WE SHOULD BE STOPPING FOR SNACKS RIGHT NOW.
YOU...
CHILLS
KYOKO AND SHIORI, YOU STAY HERE.
NOD
NOD
NOD
I CAN'T FIND SOSUKE.
ONO AND HOOKY, CAN YOU LOOK FOR HIM OVER THERE?
I KNOW THERE'S LOTS TO DO, BUT...
STOP FOOLING AROUND, WILL YOU?!
SOSUKE?

COME ON!
K-THUNK

EEEEEK!
SUDDENLY!
ガビーン!

WHAT THE HECK IS IT THIS TIME?

FWOOO

HEH HEH. I NEVER THOUGHT I'D SEE YOU HERE!
THANKS TO YOU, MY PRIDE AS A WARRIOR ELITE WAS CRUSHED...

See Mission 19

BAM
WHAAAA?!
BWOING

HMPH. I'LL JUST USE MY KNIFE TO...

SOSUKE, ARE YOU AL-RIGHT?
SHH!
THERE ARE MORE OF THEM. BE CAREFUL.

GRAGH!
THWUMP!

BUT IT'S DANGEROUS HERE! WE HAVE TO GET AWAY!
I DON'T WANT ANYTHING TO HAPPEN TO THE OTHERS!

TOO LATE!

FWUP

FWUP

FWUP

SHWIP

BAM

STAND BACK, CHIDORI!
R... RIGHT!
HERE I COME!
SHA-CHING!
FWUP
FWUP
HMPF!
RUNNING AWAY AGAIN, EH?
SHWUP
SHWUP
SHWUP

AND **YOU'RE** WALKING RIGHT INTO...

TWACK

THE **TRAP** THAT I SET!!

PA-KOWW

GWAA!

I SET IT JUST IN CASE. IT CAME IN HANDY AFTER ALL...
THP THP THP
PSHHHH
GRIP
IRON FIST ?!
CRACK!
WAAAAA!
We came to the mountains and found MONSTERS!
うわあああん
山には魔物がいるっ
LET'S GO!
KYOKO AND THEM HAVE NOTHING TO DO WITH THIS, BUT HE...
STUPID COLOR-BY-NUMBERS BAD GUY!
THEY'RE ALL GONE.
I DON'T SEE THEIR LUGGAGE, EITHER...

YOU AGAIN?!
ぶら〜ん
SWAY
OF ALL THE DIRTY TRICKS...!
WHAT HAPPENED TO THE **KIDS** WHO WERE HERE?
THEY RAN AWAY AFTER THEY SAW ME CAUGHT IN THIS TRAP! MORON.
WATCH YOUR MOUTH!
FWACK!
GRH!
I'VE FOUND OUR POSITION ON THE GPS...
BUT THE PROBLEM IS LOCATING THE **HOUSE.**
THAT MAP PUT IT SOME-WHERE TO THE NORTH.
THEY MIGHT'VE HEADED TO THE HOUSE!
WE HAVE TO CATCH UP TO THEM!
YEAH.
HM.
LET'S JUST FOLLOW THE PATH FOR NOW.

SOSUKE?
HOW COME YOU'RE NOT TIRED? WE'VE BEEN WALKING FOR TWO HOURS STRAIGHT.
?
DO YOU WANT TO TAKE A BREAK?
YEAH,
KIND OF.
SLIIINK
GAAAUGH!
SLITHER
SLITHER
SLITHER
HMM.
A SNAKE'S NEST, EH?
SHOULD WE USE THEM AS FOOD?
DANGLE
NO WAY!
I'M NOT EATIN' THAT!
LET'S KEEP MOVING!
GOOSEBUMPS
SNATCH
SNATCH
SNATCH
THERE'S THREE DIFFERENT PATHS. WHICH ONE SHOULD WE TAKE?
THE LEFT.
THE RIGHT ONE GOES DOWN A LITTLE.

I SEE.

I GUESS YOUR SURVIVAL SKILLS ARE FINALLY COMING IN HANDY.

YOU THINK SO?

YAAAAUGH!

SLIDE

SLIDE

SLIDE

GRAB

SLIP

AAUGH!
SHAAA

CHIDORI! GO INTO THAT CAVE!
OK!

UGH, I'M SOAKED!
EEK!
HERE.
DRY OFF BEFORE YOUR BODY TEMPER-ATURE DROPS.

SHAAA

I'M COLD.

YOU'LL CATCH A COLD DRESSED LIKE THAT.
USE THIS SLEEPING BAG TO KEEP WARM.
THANKS.
YOU BROUGHT THAT, TOO?
RUSTLE

WE COULD BE HELD UP HERE FOR UP TO AN HOUR.
WE SHOULD REST AND SAVE UP OUR STRENGTH.
SIGH
ぬく ぬく
WARM AND COMFY

SOSUKE...
I'M REALLY TIRED. DO YOU MIND IF I TAKE A LITTLE NAP?
DROOP

NO PROBLEM.
YOU LOOK EVEN MORE TIRED THAN BEFORE. ARE YOU OKAY?
SORRY, BUT CAN I USE YOU FOR A PILLOW?
UH-HUH.
SURE.

Whenever I'm with Sosuke,
I feel useless, but...

At times like these…
I'm glad he's the one that is with me.

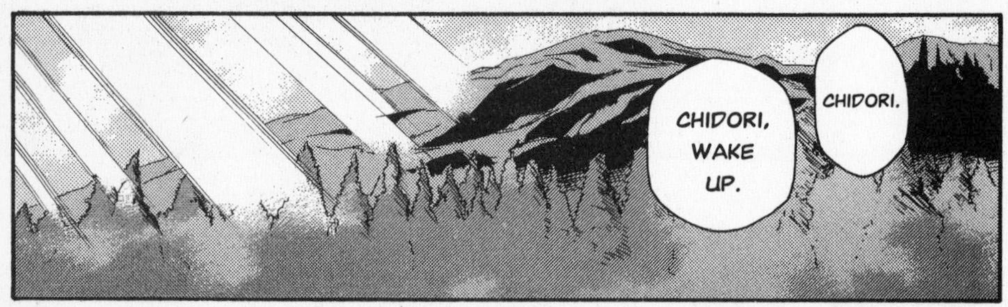

WHA?

WAS I ASLEEP LONG?

THE RAIN JUST STOPPED.

AND IT LOOKS LIKE THE HOUSE IS RIGHT OVER **THERE.**

It was hidden by the clouds.

WHAAAA?

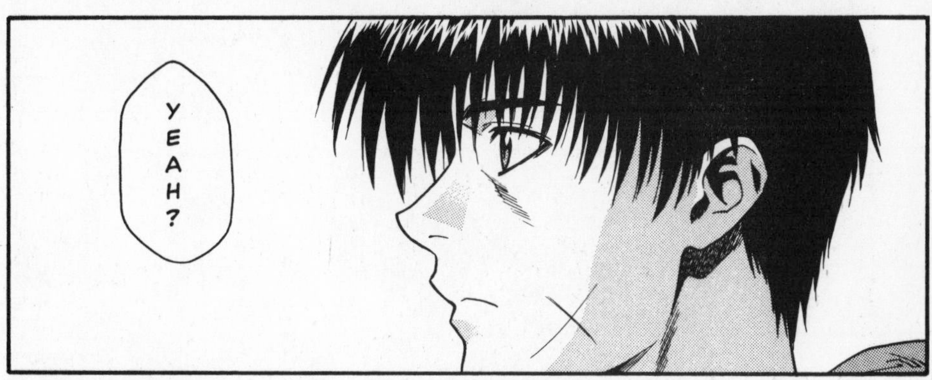

DO YOU GET THE FEELING THAT WE REALLY MISSED OUT ON SOMETHING?

YOU'RE IMAGINING THINGS.

Hey, hey! There's not enough meat on there!

AHAHAHAHA

SIZZLE SIZZLE

Continued in Volume ⑥

Special Project: Taiwan Manga, an Exclusive Report
First time flying business class
URGENT REPORT: TAIWAN TRAVEL LOG
HELLO! THIS IS TAKEO, REPORTING TO YOU FROM SOMEWHERE UP IN THE CLOUDS.
BACK IN AUGUST, I WENT TO TAIWAN ON BUSINESS.
AND SO (WITH A LITTLE HELP FROM MR."SU") I'M PROUD TO PRESENT MY "MANGA FAIR IN TAIPEI,"
AND "TAIWAN CULTURE IS TOO FRICKIN' COOL" ADVENTURES!
SNORE
FIRST, WE WENT FROM THE AIRPORT TO OUR HOTEL VIA HIRED CAR.
THERE'S NO EXPRESSWAY TOLL HERE, SO IT WAS A REALLY SMOOTH RIDE.
Not like Japan at all.
WHOA!
SNORE
WHAT THE HECK IS ALL THIS?
LINED UP!
Those scooters can weave right between cars, but space can get pretty tight. Sometimes, they brush up against the cars!
If you asked someone, they'd say "The only people who ride bikes are poor people and Americans." The streets are filled with scooters. Even the POLICE ride scooters.
IT ALMOST LOOKS LIKE THEY'RE LINED UP FOR A RACE!
COOL
IS THIS WHY THERE ARE SO MANY BEAT-UP CARS?
WOKE UP
AFTER CHECKING IN, WE VISITED THE EDITORIAL DIVISION OF KADOKAWA'S TAIWAN OFFICE.
Is that pronounced "su" or "shi?"
It's closer to "Su."
WE MET WITH EVERYONE WHO'D BE HELPING US OUT ON OUR STAY,
AND STUDIED A LITTLE BIT OF MANDARIN FOR THE NEXT DAY'S MANGA FAIR.
↑ Mr. Ono, who is a great editor.

By the way, at restaurants, they bring out **RICE PORRIDGE** instead of just rice. All the potato they put in it makes it taste delicious!

It makes you feel totally stuffed!

Taiwanese cooking has a lot of flavors I've never tasted before! Many dishes have a saké or salt taste to them.

The Taiwanese people seem most energetic at night.

Some stores don't get up and running until almost noon, but they'll easily stay open until 1:00 or 2:00 in the morning.

The night market is open almost every day, so it's like there's always a festival going on! ♪

Keeping those kinds of hours is enough to make a manga author jealous.

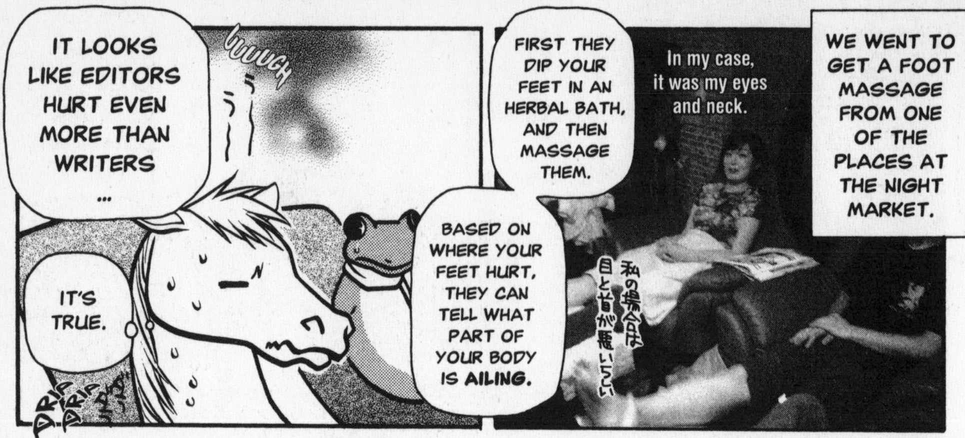

I wish there were cool rich people like that in Japan, too!

AFTER A NIGHT AT THE SPACIOUS HOTEL, IT WAS FINALLY TIME FOR WHAT WE CAME FOR IN THE FIRST PLACE ...

The atmosphere of the fair was closer to that of the **CHARACTER SHOWS** back in Japan.

But it wasn't **JUST** manga! They had DVDs, merchandise and art materials on sale there, as well as author autograph sessions and an area for playing card games!

They even sold Japanese fan comics!

During the six days the fair was held, about 100,000 people came!

200名様
Two hundred people
WELCOME!

WHEN I GOT ON STAGE, THERE WAS A RUMBLING FROM THE CROWD.

OF COURSE, THEY WERE SHOCKED TO FIND OUT THAT A WOMAN DRAWS MANGA LIKE THIS.

WHOOOAAA

おおおおお!

WHOA! THERE'S NOTHING BUT BOYS!

What'll I do if they SWARM me?

IT LOOKS LIKE THERE ARE A LOT OF PEOPLE WHO WILL BE FINDING OUT TODAY THAT YOU'RE A **WOMAN.**

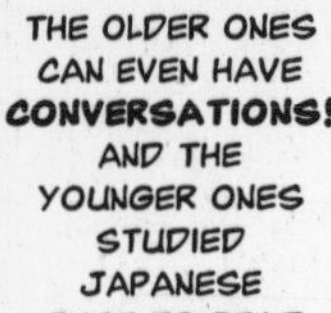

The heat and rain didn't seem to bother anyone in line; they just kept waiting there quietly. I was really impressed.

There were even some boys who said, "My girlfriend is a fan of yours, and she asked me to get your autograph." It's too cool!

No wonder she loves you!

I HEARD MR. SU'S VOICE COMING FROM SOMEWHERE.

Seems to be giving a speech about the series

When did he get up on stage?

AFTER FOUR HOURS, MY WORK WAS DONE.

TIRED OUT

Japanese

GOOD LUCK, MS. TATEO!

All my female fans are so cute!

WHEN I HEARD TWO GIRLS CHEERING ME ON, IT MADE ME HAPPY.

NEXT, WE WENT TO EAT AGAIN.

TODAY, WE'RE EATING AT "TENSHOEN," A RESTAURANT THAT SERVES SHANGHAI CUISINE!

The Japanese gang, continuing to eat & drink

I HATE TO REPEAT MYSELF, BUT EVERYTHING WAS DELICIOUS!

The tea was great, too!

I EVEN TRIED EATING FROG FOR THE FIRST TIME!

Fried, dripping with soy sauce, and spiced.

IT'S ONLY THE LEG, SO IT'LL BE PERFECTLY FINE!

ぱく

CHOMP

WOAH. IT'S INCREDIBLE!

For a moment, I saw heaven.

FROG LEGS BECAME A PART OF ME.

Happily ever after.

Thanks to everyone at the Taiwan Kadokawa office, who were all very kind. I think you helped me get over my fear of the autograph session! It was totally fun and great and hot, and it gave me a lot of energy! I think the biggest thing I'll be taking home with me from this trip is the feeling that fans are the same the world over.

The temple we visited

It only takes three hours by plane!

FULL METAL PANIC VOLUME FIVE

Translator **AMY FORSYTH**
Lead Translator/Translation Supervisor **JAVIER LOPEZ**
ADV Manga Translation Staff **KAY BERTRAND, BRENDAN FRAYNE, HARUKA KANEKO-SMITH AND EIKO McGREGOR**

Print Production/ Art Studio Manager **LISA PUCKETT**
Pre-press Manager **KLYS REEDYK**
Art Production Manager **RYAN MASON**
Sr. Designer/Creative Manager **JORGE ALVARADO**
Graphic Designer/Group Leader **SHANNON RASBERRY**
Graphic Designer **HEATHER GARY AND CHY LING**
Graphic Artists **KRISTINA MILESKI, NATALIA MORALES, CHRIS LAPP AND NANAKO TSUKIHASHI**
Graphic Intern **MARK MEZA**

International Coordinator **TORU IWAKAMI**
International Coordinator **ATSUSHI KANBAYASHI**

Publishing Editor **SUSAN ITIN**
Assistant Editor **MARGARET SCHAROLD**
Editorial Assistant **VARSHA BHUCHAR**
Proofreader **SHERIDAN JACOBS**

Research/ Traffic Coordinator **MARSHA ARNOLD**

Executive V.P., CFO, COO **KEVIN CORCORAN**

President, C.E.O & Publisher **JOHN LEDFORD**

Email: editor@adv-manga.com
www.adv-manga.com
www.advfilms.com

For sales and distribution inquiries please call **1.800.282.7202**

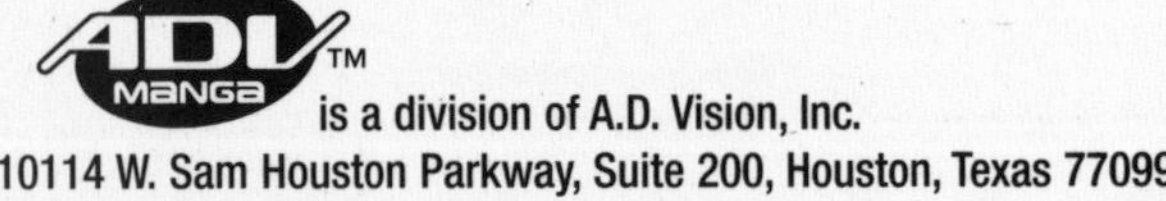

is a division of A.D. Vision, Inc.
10114 W. Sam Houston Parkway, Suite 200, Houston, Texas 77099

ISBN: 1-4139-0051-8
First printing, June 2004
10 9 8 7 6 5 4 3 2 1
Printed in Canada

Dear Reader,

On behalf of the ADV Manga translation team, thank you for purchasing an ADV book. We are enthusiastic and committed to our work, and strive to carry our enthusiasm over into the book you hold in your hands.

Our goal is to retain the spirit of the original Japanese book. While great care has been taken to render a true and accurate translation, some cultural or readability issues may require a line to be adapted for greater accessibility to our readers. At times, manga titles that include culturally-specific concepts will feature a "Translator's Notes" section, which explains noteworthy references to the original text.

We hope our commitment to a faithful translation is evident in every ADV book you purchase.

Sincerely,

Madoka Moroe

Haruka Kaneko-Smith

Javier Lopez
Lead Translator

Eiko McGregor

Kay Bertrand

ADV MANGA™

Brendan Frayne

Amy Forsyth

Full Metal Panic! Vol 05

PG. 56 **What IS this thing, Friday?**
Friday is the name of Mao's AS unit's AI.

PG. 121 **Chameleon plant**
Called *dokudami* in Japanese, the chameleon plant is native to Japan and a staple of herbal remedies. It has a variety of uses, including a diuretic and an anti-inflammatory.

PG. 134 **It's summer, but I can hear nightingales. Along with the cicadas.**
Nightingales are usually most abundant during the spring, which is why the character remarks about hearing them in summer. Cicadas, however, are symbolic of summer in Japan.

PG. 137 **If we were in the Matrix...**
What Kaname said in the original Japanese was that if they were in the Matrix, she'd install *Tokimeki Memorial* into Sosuke's thick skull. *Tokimeki Memorial* is a "love simulation game" where, as the protagonist, you must try to win the heart of no less than a dozen girls, culminating in a date with a character (coincidentally?) named Shiori. Presumably, Kaname was implying that Sosuke could stand to learn a thing or three about women.

PG. 138 **I feel like I'm in a C.W. Nichol novel!**
C.W. Nichol is a novelist and environmental activist. He is also the author of *Moving Zen*, which chronicles his journal to spiritual quietude through the study of karate.

Page 2 Translator's Notes Continued...

PG. 156 **Kadokawa**
The publishing giant that puts out the *Full Metal Panic!* graphic novels in Japan.

PG. 157 **It's like a bigger version of Ameyoko back in Japan!**
Ameyoko is a busy market street located along the Yamanote line between Okachimachi and Ueno. The name may be short for *Ameya Yokocho* ("candy store alley"), because traditionally, candy was sold there. Conversely, *Ame* could also be short for "America," because this street was the site of a black market in American goods after WWII. Nowadays, all kinds of goods are available there for bargain prices.

(1) Inside, there were people SITTING DOWN and reading!
In Japan, the order of the day is *tachiyomi*, or standing and reading. Sitting down is unheard of, as such behavior is considered dirty and highly frowned upon.

(2) Character shows
Conventions spotlighting anime/manga characters. The most common guests include the voice actors and actresses who worked on the animated versions.

(3) They even sold Japanese fan comics!
The original Japanese term was *dojinshi*. These so-called "fan comics" are (you guessed it) drawn by fans and often involve the characters and situations of professionally published manga. While there are of course exceptions to every rule, *dojinsh* tend to be rather racy in their content.

LETTTER FROM THE EDITOR

Dear Reader,

Thank you for purchasing an ADV Manga book. We hope you enjoyed the excitement of *Full Metal Panic!*, volume five.

It is our sincere commitment in reproducing Asian comics and graphic novels to retain as much of the character of the original book as possible. From the right-to-left format of the Japanese books to the meaning of the story in the original language, the ADV Manga team is working hard to publish a quality book for our fans and readers. Write to us with your questions or comments, and tell us how you liked this and other ADV books. Be sure to visit our website at www.adv-manga.com and view the list of upcoming titles, sign up for special announcements, and fill out our survey.

The ADV Manga team of translators, designers, graphic artists, production managers, traffic managers, and editors hope you will buy more ADV books–there's a lot more in store from ADV Manga!

www.adv-manga.com

Publishing Editor	Assistant Editor	Editorial Assistant
Susan B. Itin	Margaret Scharold	Varsha Bhuchar

More Manga Monthly!

Aria vol. 1	ISBN 1-4139-0040-2	$ 9.99
Azumanga Daioh vol. 1	ISBN 1-4139-0000-3	$ 9.99
Azumanga Daioh vol. 2	ISBN 1-4139-0023-2	$ 9.99
Azumanga Daioh vol. 3	ISBN 1-4139-0030-5	$ 9.99
Azumanga Daioh vol. 4	ISBN 1-4139-0048-8	$ 9.99
Blue Inferior vol. 1	ISBN 1-4139-0086-0	$ 9.99
Chrono Crusade vol. 1	ISBN 1-4139-0084-4	$ 9.99
Darkside Blues	ISBN 1-4139-0002-X	$14.98
Demon City Hunter vol. 1	ISBN 1-4139-0003-8	$ 9.99
Demon City Hunter vol. 2	ISBN 1-4139-0025-9	$ 9.99
Demon City Shinjuku vol. 1	ISBN 1-4139-0004-6	$ 9.99
Demon City Shinjuku vol. 2	ISBN 1-4139-0028-3	$ 9.99
Demon Palace Babylon vol. 1	ISBN 1-4139-0005-4	$ 9.99
Demon Palace Babylon vol. 2	ISBN 1-4139-0029-1	$ 9.99
Desert Coral vol. 1	ISBN 1-4139-0050-X	$ 9.99
Fantasy Land vol. 1	ISBN 1-4139-0066-6	$ 9.99
Figure 17 vol. 1	ISBN 1-4139-0019-4	$ 9.99
Figure 17 vol. 2	ISBN 1-4139-0041-0	$ 9.99
Full Metal Panic! vol. 1	ISBN 1-4139-0001-1	$ 9.99
Full Metal Panic! vol. 2	ISBN 1-4139-0006-2	$ 9.99
Full Metal Panic! vol. 3	ISBN 1-4139-0007-0	$ 9.99
Full Metal Panic! vol. 4	ISBN 1-4139-0039-9	$ 9.99
Full Metal Panic! vol. 5	ISBN 1-4139-0051-8	$ 9.99
Full Metal Panic! Film Book	ISBN 1-4139-0027-5	$19.98
Gunslinger Girl vol. 1	ISBN 1-4139-0020-8	$ 9.99
Happy Lesson vol. 1	ISBN 1-4139-0021-6	$ 9.99

ANIME • MANGA • VIDEO GAMES • TOYS • MOVIES •
IF IT'S COOL, YOU'LL FIND IT EACH AND EVERY MONTH IN THE PAGES OF NEWTYPE USA, ALONG WITH FREE DVDS, POSTERS, POSTCARDS AND MUCH, MUCH MORE.
Newtype USA
THE MOVING PICTURES MAGAZINE.
月刊ニュータイプ
米国版
IT BEGINS WHERE OTHER MAGAZINES END •

MANGA SURVEY

PLEASE MAIL THE COMPLETED FORM TO: EDITOR – ADV MANGA
c/o A.D. Vision, Inc. 10114 W. Sam Houston Pkwy., Suite 200 Houston, TX 77099

Name: ______________________________

Address: ______________________________

City, State, Zip: ______________________________

____

E-Mail: ______________________________

Male ☐ Female ☐ Age: ______________________________

☐ ***CHECK HERE IF YOU WOULD LIKE TO RECEIVE OTHER INFORMATION OR FUTURE OFFERS FROM ADV.***

All information provided will be used for internal purposes only. We promise not to sell or otherwise divulge your information.

1. Annual Household Income (*Check only one*)

☐ Under $25,000
☐ $25,000 to $50,000
☐ $50,000 to $75,000
☐ Over $75,000

2. How do you hear about new Manga releases? (*Check all that apply*)

☐ Browsing in Store
☐ Internet Reviews
☐ Anime News Websites
☐ Direct Email Campaigns
☐ Online forums (message boards and chat rooms)
☐ Carrier pigeon
☐ Other: ______________________________
☐ Magazine Ad
☐ Online Advertising
☐ Conventions
☐ TV Advertising

3. Which magazines do you read? (*Check all that apply*)

☐ Wizard
☐ SPIN
☐ Animerica
☐ Rolling Stone
☐ Maxim
☐ DC Comics
☐ URB
☐ Polygon
☐ Original Play Station Magazine
☐ Entertainment Weekly
☐ YRB
☐ EGM
☐ Newtype USA
☐ SciFi
☐ Starlog
☐ Wired
☐ Vice
☐ BPM
☐ I hate reading
☐ Other: ______________

4. Have you visited the ADV Manga website?
- ☐ Yes
- ☐ No

5. Have you made any manga purchases online from the ADV website?
- ☐ Yes
- ☐ No

6. If you have visited the ADV Manga website, how would you rate your online experience?
- ☐ Excellent
- ☐ Good
- ☐ Average
- ☐ Poor

7. What genre of manga do you prefer?
(*Check all that apply*)
- ☐ adventure
- ☐ romance
- ☐ detective
- ☐ action
- ☐ horror
- ☐ sci-fi/fantasy
- ☐ sports
- ☐ comedy

8. How many manga titles have you purchased in the last 6 months?
- ☐ none
- ☐ 1-4
- ☐ 5-10
- ☐ 11+

9. Where do you make your manga purchases? (*Check all that apply*)
- ☐ comic store
- ☐ bookstore
- ☐ newsstand
- ☐ online
- ☐ other:________________
- ☐ department store
- ☐ grocery store
- ☐ video store
- ☐ video game store

10. Which bookstores do you usually make your manga purchases at?
(*Check all that apply*)
- ☐ Barnes & Noble
- ☐ Walden Books
- ☐ Suncoast
- ☐ Best Buy
- ☐ Amazon.com
- ☐ Borders
- ☐ Books-A-Million
- ☐ Toys "Я" Us
- ☐ Other bookstore: ____________________

11. What's your favorite anime/manga website? (*Check all that apply*)
- ☐ adv-manga.com
- ☐ advfilms.com
- ☐ rightstuf.com
- ☐ animenewsservice.com
- ☐ animenewsnetwork.com
- ☐ Other:________________
- ☐ animeondvd.com
- ☐ anipike.com
- ☐ animeonline.net
- ☐ planetanime.com
- ☐ animenation.com